What Would Dickens Do?

WHAT WOULD DICKENS DO?

Summersdale Publishers Ltd
46 West Street
Chichester
West Sussex
PO19 1RP
UK

www.summersdale.com

Printed and bound by
CPI Group (UK) Ltd, Croydon, CR0 4YY

ISBN: 978-1-84953-252-5

What Would **Dickens** Do?

Constance Moore

summersdale

Contents

INTRODUCTION

When life gets difficult and we find ourselves in need of guidance, it's often hard to know who to turn to. When friends can't provide the answers to our dilemmas, sometimes we find ourselves turning to the great inspirational thinkers from past eras.

Charles Dickens is one such person. Considered by many to be the greatest author of the Victorian period, he rose from humble beginnings and poverty to a position of great influence and respect. His work represented and cultivated the conscience of Victorian England, dealing with social issues big and small with a rigour and humour that still resonates today in the twenty-first century.

Reflecting the experiences of his life, Dickens' writing encompasses many themes and settings, from child poverty to the convoluted British legal system to the conflicts of family life. From his debut novel, *The Pickwick Papers*, up to the unfinished and posthumously published *The Mystery of Edwin Drood*, Charles Dickens' work offers an unmatched combination of humour, intrigue and pathos, and insight into the human condition.

With this in mind, what better author could there be to guide us through the trials and tribulations of everyday (and not-so-everyday) life? Who else is there who can teach us the benefits of being a madman, how to gain a free meal with rhetoric and why one should never visit the county town of Essex?

> That was a memorable day to me, for it made great changes in me. But, it is the same with any life. Imagine one selected day struck out of it, and think how different its course would have been. Pause you who read this, and think for the moment of the long chain of iron or gold, of thorns or flowers, that would never have bound you, but for the formation of the first link on one memorable day.
>
> *GREAT EXPECTATIONS*

Every day is precious and every decision possibly life-changing. So why not take a moment and ask yourself: What Would Dickens Do?

FRIENDSHIP

How may one tactfully express
one's views on a friend's
choice of husband?

'Mr Quilp may be a very nice man,' said this
lady, 'and I supposed there's no doubt he is,
because Mrs Quilp says he is, and Mrs Jiniwin
says he is, and they ought to know, or nobody
does. But still he is not quite a – what one
calls a handsome man, nor quite a young
man neither, which might be a little excuse
for him if anything could be; whereas his
wife is young, and is good-looking, and is a
woman – which is the greatest thing after all.'

THE OLD CURIOSITY SHOP, A FRIEND OF MRS QUILP'S

Alternatively, how may one most easily express one's wholehearted opinion on the matter?

'He is the greatest tyrant that ever lived, she daren't call her soul her own, he makes her tremble with a word and even with a look, he frightens her to death, and she hasn't the spirit to give him a word back, no, not a single word.'

THE OLD CURIOSITY SHOP, MRS QUILP'S MOTHER

And what words can an unkind husband use to stop his wife meeting with her friends?

'If ever you listen to these beldames again, I'll bite you.'

THE OLD CURIOSITY SHOP, MR QUILP

What's more important in a letter from a friend: good spelling or a sincerely expressed greeting?

'MI DEER JO i OPE U R KR WITE WELL i OPE i SHAL SON B HABELL 4 2 TEEDGE U JO AN THEN WE SHORL B SO GLODD AN WEN i M PRENGTD 2 U JO WOT LARX AN BLEVE ME INF XN PIP.'

GREAT EXPECTATIONS, LETTER FROM PIP PIRRIP TO JOE GARGERY

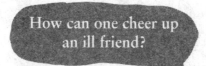

How can one cheer up
an ill friend?

I grieve to hear that you have been ill, but I
hope that the spring, when it comes, will find
you blooming with the rest of the flowers.

LETTER TO MRS HOGGE, 14 APRIL 1858

What's the best way to have a good time with friends?

'Fan the sinking flame of hilarity with the wing of friendship; and pass the rosy wine.'

THE OLD CURIOSITY SHOP, DICK SWIVELLER

What is a good way to react to friendship between your beloved and your best friend?

'Esther, it's enough to make anybody but me jealous,' said Caddy, laughing and shaking her head; 'but it only makes me joyful, for you are the first friend I ever had, and the best friend I ever can have, and nobody can respect and love you too much to please me.'

BLEAK HOUSE

LOVE AND MARRIAGE

Is love a pleasure or a torment?

'I never had one hour's happiness in her society, and yet my mind all round the four-and-twenty hours was harping on the happiness of having her with me unto death.'

GREAT EXPECTATIONS, PIP PIRRIP

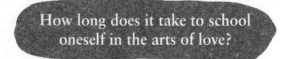

How long does it take to school oneself in the arts of love?

There is no school in which a pupil gets on so fast, as that in which Kit became a scholar when he gave Barbara the kiss. He saw what Barbara meant now – he had his lesson by heart all at once – she was the book – there it was before him, as plain as print.

THE OLD CURIOSITY SHOP

Is it true that wives
obey their husbands?

'... the law supposes that your wife
acts under your direction.'

'If the law supposes that,' said Mr Bumble,
squeezing his hat emphatically in both hands,
'the law is a ass – a idiot. If that's the eye
of the law, the law is a bachelor; and the
worst I wish the law is, that his eye may be
opened by experience – by experience.'

OLIVER TWIST

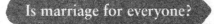

Is marriage for everyone?

All the housemaid hopes is, happiness for
'em – marriage is a lottery, and the more
she thinks about it, the more she feels the
independence and the safety of a single life.

DOMBEY AND SON

If one were to become an articulator of bones and a taxidermist, would it affect one's chances with women?

'The lady is a going to give her 'and where she has already given her 'art, next Monday.'

'Then the lady's objection has been met?' said Silas.

'Mr Wegg,' said Venus, 'as I did name to you, I think, on a former occasion, if not on former occasions... what the nature of the lady's objection was, I may impart, without violating any of the tender confidences since sprung up between the lady and myself, how it has been met, through the kind interference of two good friends of mine: one, previously acquainted with the lady: and one, not. The pint was thrown out, sir, by those two friends when they did me the great service of waiting on the lady to try if a union betwixt the lady and me could not be brought to bear... whether if, after marriage, I confined myself to the articulation of men, children, and the lower animals, it might not relieve the lady's mind of her feeling respecting being as a lady – regarded in a bony light. It was a happy thought, sir, and it took root.'

OUR MUTUAL FRIEND, MR VENUS

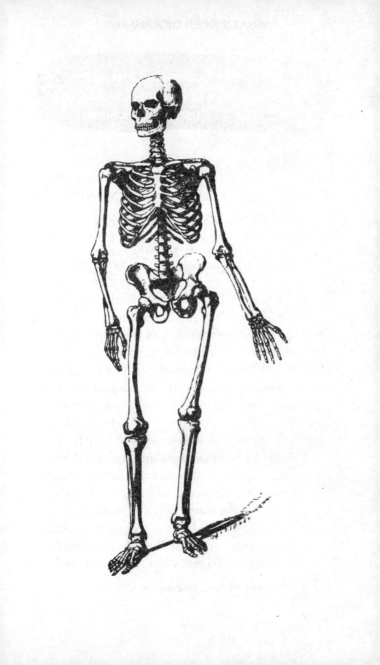

> Is it a good idea to meddle in
> the love lives of others?

'Hear me, Pip! I adopted her, to be
loved. I bred her and educated her, to be
loved. I developed her into what she is,
that she might be loved. Love her!'

She said the word often enough, and there could
be no doubt that she meant to say it; but if the
often repeated word had been hate instead of
love – despair – revenge – dire death – it could
not have sounded from her lips more like a curse.

GREAT EXPECTATIONS, MISS HAVISHAM

> How can one propose, concisely?

'Barkis is willin'!'

DAVID COPPERFIELD, MR BARKIS

How can one successfully clarify
one's matrimonial intentions?

'How should you like to be my
number two, Nelly?'

'To be what, sir?'

'My number two, Nelly, my second,
my Mrs Quilp,' said the dwarf.

The child looked frightened, but seemed not to
understand him, which Mr Quilp observing,
hastened to make his meaning more distinctly.

'To be Mrs Quilp the second, when Mrs Quilp
the first is dead, sweet Nell,' said Quilp, wrinkling
up his eyes and luring her towards him with his
bent forefinger, 'to be my wife, my little cherry-
cheeked, red-lipped wife. Say that Mrs Quilp
lives five year, or only four, you'll be just the
proper age for me. Ha ha! Be a good girl, Nelly,
a very good girl, and see if one of these days you
don't come to be Mrs Quilp of Tower Hill.'

THE OLD CURIOSITY SHOP

> How may a young woman, clearly and beyond doubt, reject a man's proposal?

'But what I have declared, I take my stand by. I cannot recall the avowal of my earnest and deep attachment to you, and I do not recall it.'

'I reject it, sir,' said Bella.

'I should be blind and deaf if I were not prepared for the reply. Forgive my offence, for it carries its punishment with it.'

'What punishment?' asked Bella.

'Is my present endurance none? But excuse me; I did not mean to cross-examine you again.'

'You take advantage of a hasty word of mine,' said Bella with a little sting of self-reproach, 'to make me seem – I don't know what. I spoke without consideration when I used it. If that was bad, I am sorry; but you repeat it after consideration, and that seems to me to be at least no better. For the rest, I beg it may be understood, Mr Rokesmith, that there is an end of this between us, now and for ever.'

'Now and for ever,' he repeated.

OUR MUTUAL FRIEND, BELLA WILFER AND JOHN ROKESMITH

> Are parents always vexed
> when their children reject
> an 'ideal' partner?

'Ma, I always hated and detested
Mr Quale!' sobbed Caddy.

'Caddy, Caddy!' returned Mrs Jellyby, opening
another letter with the greatest complacency.
'I have no doubt you did. How could you
do otherwise, being totally destitute of the
sympathies with which he overflows! Now, if my
public duties were not a favourite child to me,
if I were not occupied with large measures on
a vast scale, these petty details might grieve me
very much, Miss Summerson. But can I permit the
film of a silly proceeding on the part of Caddy
(from whom I expect nothing else) to interpose
between me and the great African continent?
No. No,' repeated Mrs Jellyby in a calm clear
voice, and with an agreeable smile, as she opened
more letters and sorted them. 'No, indeed.'

BLEAK HOUSE

What is the best way
to deal with rejection?

'She's a very charming and delightful
creature,' quoth Mr Robert Sawyer, in reply;
'and has only one fault that I know of, Ben.
It happens, unfortunately, that that single
blemish is a want of taste. She don't like me.'

THE PICKWICK PAPERS

How may a young lady
avoid kissing the man she
has been promised to?

'You're very welcome, Eddy. There! I'm sure
that's nice. Shake hands. No, I can't kiss you,
because I've got an acidulated drop in my mouth.'

THE MYSTERY OF EDWIN DROOD, ROSA BUD

What traps lurk in an innocent
conversation about the hiring
of a manservant?

'Do you think it a much greater expense
to keep two people, than to keep one?'

'La, Mr Pickwick,' said Mrs Bardell,
colouring up to the very border of her cap,
as she fancied she observed a species of
matrimonial twinkle in the eyes of her lodger;
'La, Mr Pickwick, what a question!'

'Well, but do you?' inquired Mr Pickwick.

'That depends,' said Mrs Bardell, approaching the
duster very near to Mr Pickwick's elbow which
was planted on the table. 'That depends a good
deal upon the person, you know, Mr Pickwick;
and whether it's a saving and careful person, sir.'

'That's very true,' said Mr Pickwick, 'but the
person I have in my eye (here he looked very hard
at Mrs Bardell) I think possesses these qualities;
and has, moreover, a considerable knowledge of
the world, and a great deal of sharpness, Mrs
Bardell, which may be of material use to me.'

'La, Mr Pickwick,' said Mrs Bardell, the
crimson rising to her cap-border again.

'I do,' said Mr Pickwick, growing energetic, as was his wont in speaking of a subject which interested him – 'I do, indeed; and to tell you the truth, Mrs Bardell, I have made up my mind.'

'Dear me, sir,' exclaimed Mrs Bardell.

'You'll think it very strange now,' said the amiable Mr Pickwick, with a good-humoured glance at his companion, 'that I never consulted you about this matter, and never even mentioned it, till I sent your little boy out this morning – eh?'

Mrs Bardell could only reply by a look. She had long worshipped Mr Pickwick at a distance, but here she was, all at once, raised to a pinnacle to which her wildest and most extravagant hopes had never dared to aspire. Mr Pickwick was going to propose – a deliberate plan, too – sent her little boy to the Borough, to get him out of the way – how thoughtful – how considerate!

THE PICKWICK PAPERS

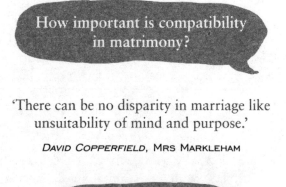

How important is compatibility
in matrimony?

'There can be no disparity in marriage like
unsuitability of mind and purpose.'

DAVID COPPERFIELD, MRS MARKLEHAM

Is marriage worth it?

'Ven you're a married man, Samivel, you'll
understand a good many things as you don't
understand now; but vether it's worth while goin'
through so much, to learn so little, as the charity-
boy said ven he got to the end of the alphabet,
is a matter o' taste. I rayther think it isn't.'

THE PICKWICK PAPERS, TONY WELLER

FAMILY

Is it necessary to mince one's words
when talking about one's in-laws?

'... if I were to develop my views to that
assembled group, they would possibly be found
of an offensive nature: my impression being that
your family are, in the aggregate, impertinent
Snobs; and, in detail, unmitigated Ruffians.'

DAVID COPPERFIELD, WILKINS MICAWBER

Is it always easy to cope
with one's own parents?

'Ma,' said Bella, angrily, 'you force me to
say that I am truly sorry I did come home,
and that I never will come home again.'

OUR MUTUAL FRIEND, BELLA WILFER

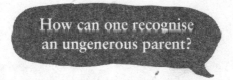

How can one recognise
an ungenerous parent?

At this command, or by this gracious permission, the lesson went on. Prince Turveydrop sometimes played the kit, dancing; sometimes played the piano, standing; sometimes hummed the tune with what little breath he could spare, while he set a pupil right; always conscientiously moved with the least proficient through every step and every part of the figure; and never rested for an instant. His distinguished father did nothing whatever but stand before the fire, a model of deportment.

'And he never does anything else,' said the old lady of the censorious countenance. 'Yet would you believe that it's HIS name on the door-plate?'

'His son's name is the same, you know,' said I.

'He wouldn't let his son have any name if he could take it from him,' returned the old lady. 'Look at the son's dress!' It certainly was plain – threadbare – almost shabby. 'Yet the father must be garnished and tricked out,' said the old lady, 'because of his deportment. I'd deport him! Transport him would be better!'

BLEAK HOUSE

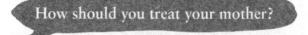

How should you treat your mother?

'The time will come, my boy,' pursues the trooper, 'when this hair of your mother's will be grey, and this forehead all crossed and re-crossed with wrinkles, and a fine old lady she'll be then. Take care, while you are young, that you can think in those days, "I never whitened a hair of her dear head – I never marked a sorrowful line in her face!"'

BLEAK HOUSE, MATTHEW BAGNET

Is pride ever acceptable?

Pride is one of the seven deadly sins; but it cannot be the pride of a mother in her children, for that is a compound of two cardinal virtues – faith and hope.

NICHOLAS NICKLEBY

Sticks and stones can injure bones, but how should one respond to hurtful words?

'If oaths, or prayers, or words, could rid me of you, they should. I would be quit of you, and would be relieved if you were dead.'

'I know it,' returned the other. 'I said so, didn't I? But neither oaths, or prayers, nor words, WILL kill me, and therefore I live, and mean to live.'

'And his mother died!' cried the old man, passionately clasping his hands and looking upward; 'and this is Heaven's justice!'

THE OLD CURIOSITY SHOP, FREDERICK TRENT AND HIS GRANDFATHER

Or is it better to make peace, not war?

'It's a devil of a thing, gentlemen,' said Mr Swiveller, 'when relations fall out and disagree. If the wing of friendship should never moult a feather, the wing of relationship should never be clipped, but be always expanded and serene. Why should a grandson and grandfather peg away at each other with mutual wiolence when all might be bliss and concord. Why not jine hands and forgit it?'

THE OLD CURIOSITY SHOP, DICK SWIVELLER

> Is it a pleasant thing to be an older brother?

Wherever childhood congregated to play, there was little Moloch making Johnny fag and toil. Wherever Johnny desired to stay, little Moloch became fractious, and would not remain. Whenever Johnny wanted to go out, Moloch was asleep, and must be watched. Whenever Johnny wanted to stay at home, Moloch was awake, and must be taken out. Yet Johnny was verily persuaded that it was a faultless baby, without its peer in the realm of England, and was quite content to catch meek glimpses of things in general from behind its skirts, or over its limp flapping bonnet, and to go staggering about with it like a very little porter with a very large parcel, which was not directed to anybody, and could never be delivered anywhere.

THE HAUNTED MAN AND THE GHOST'S BARGAIN

What about being an older sister?

'Do you know that he is worth fifty of you?'

'It may easily be so, Charley,
but I cannot marry him.'

'You mean that you are conscious that you can't
appreciate him, and don't deserve him, I suppose?'

'I mean that I do not like him, Charley,
and that I will never marry him.'

'Upon my soul,' exclaimed the boy, 'you are a
nice picture of a sister! Upon my soul, you are a
pretty piece of disinterestedness! And so all my
endeavours to cancel the past and to raise myself
in the world, and to raise you with me, are to be
beaten down by YOUR low whims; are they?'

'I will not reproach you, Charley.'

'Hear her!' exclaimed the boy, looking round
at the darkness. 'She won't reproach me! She
does her best to destroy my fortunes and her
own, and she won't reproach me! Why, you'll
tell me, next, that you won't reproach Mr
Headstone for coming out of the sphere to
which he is an ornament, and putting himself
at YOUR feet, to be rejected by YOU!'

'No, Charley; I will only tell you, as I told
himself, that I thank him for doing so,
that I am sorry he did so, and that I hope
he will do much better, and be happy.'

OUR MUTUAL FRIEND, CHARLEY AND LIZZIE HEXAM

CHILDREN

Are children's hearts naturally kind?

'Treachery don't come natural to beaming
youth; but trust and pity, love and
constancy, – they do, thank God!'

MRS LIRRIPER'S LEGACY, MRS LIRRIPER

Or is the opposite the case?

Mrs Hubble shook her head, and contemplating
me with a mournful presentiment that I
should come to no good, asked, 'Why is
it that the young are never grateful?' This
moral mystery seemed too much for the
company until Mr Hubble tersely solved it
by saying, 'Naterally wicious.' Everybody
then murmured 'True!' and looked at me in a
particularly unpleasant and personal manner.

GREAT EXPECTATIONS

Should children be treated fairly?

It may be only small injustice that the child
can be exposed to; but the child is small,
and its world is small, and its rocking-
horse stands as many hands high, according
to scale, as a big-boned Irish hunter.

GREAT EXPECTATIONS

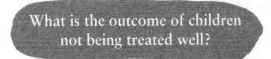

**What is the outcome of children
not being treated well?**

In a school carried on by sheer cruelty,
whether it is presided over by a dunce or
not, there is not likely to be much learnt.

DAVID COPPERFIELD

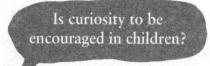

Is curiosity to be encouraged in children?

'I tell you what, young fellow,' said she, 'I didn't bring you up by hand to badger people's lives out. It would be blame to me and not praise, if I had. People are put in the Hulks because they murder, and because they rob, and forge, and do all sorts of bad; and they always begin by asking questions. Now, you get along to bed!'

GREAT EXPECTATIONS, MRS JOE

Is it better for the young to talk, or to listen?

'Silence, sir!' returned his father, 'what do you mean by talking, when you see people that are more than two or three times your age, sitting still and silent and not dreaming of saying a word?'

'Why that's the proper time for me to talk, isn't it?' said Joe rebelliously.

'The proper time, sir!' retorted his father, 'the proper time's no time.'

'Ah to be sure!' muttered Parkes, nodding gravely to the other two who nodded likewise, observing under their breaths that that was the point.

'The proper time's no time, sir,' repeated John Willet; 'when I was your age I never talked, I never wanted to talk. I listened and improved myself that's what I did.'

BARNABY RUDGE

> What is the nature of young
> people's sensibility?

A certain institution in Mr Podsnap's mind
which he called 'the young person' may be
considered to have been embodied in Miss
Podsnap, his daughter. It was an inconvenient
and exacting institution, as requiring everything
in the universe to be filed down and fitted to
it. The question about everything was, would
it bring a blush into the cheek of the young
person? And the inconvenience of the young
person was, that, according to Mr Podsnap,
she seemed always liable to burst into blushes
when there was no need at all. There appeared
to be no line of demarcation between the young
person's excessive innocence, and another
person's guiltiest knowledge. Take Mr Podsnap's
word for it, and the soberest tints of drab,
white, lilac, and grey, were all flaming red to
this troublesome Bull of a young person.

OUR MUTUAL FRIEND

> Is it a good thing to force religion onto a child?

On summer evenings, when every flower, and tree, and bird, might have better addressed my soft young heart, I have in my day been caught in the palm of a female hand by the crown, have been violently scrubbed from the neck to the roots of the hair as a purification for the Temple, and have then been carried off highly charged with saponaceous electricity, to be steamed like a potato in the unventilated breath of the powerful Boanerges Boiler and his congregation, until what small mind I had, was quite steamed out of me.

THE UNCOMMERICAL TRAVELLER

> Why are young people so headstrong?

'David,' said Mr Murdstone, 'to the young this is a world for action; not for moping and droning in.'

DAVID COPPERFIELD, EDWARD MURDSTONE

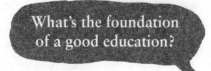

What's the foundation of a good education?

'Now, what I want is, Facts. Teach these boys and girls nothing but Facts. Facts alone are wanted in life. Plant nothing else, and root out everything else. You can only form the minds of reasoning animals upon Facts: nothing else will ever be of any service to them.'

HARD TIMES, THOMAS GRADGRIND

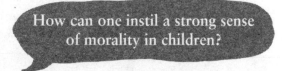

How can one instil a strong sense of morality in children?

It being a part of Mrs Pipchin's system not to encourage a child's mind to develop and expand itself like a young flower, but to open it by force like an oyster, the moral of these lessons was usually of a violent and stunning character: the hero – a naughty boy – seldom, in the mildest catastrophe, being finished off by anything less than a lion, or a bear.

DOMBEY AND SON

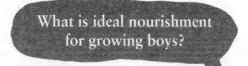

What is ideal nourishment
for growing boys?

'Oh! nonsense,' rejoined Mrs Squeers. 'If the
young man comes to be a teacher here, let
him understand, at once, that we don't want
any foolery about the boys. They have the
brimstone and treacle, partly because if they
hadn't something or other in the way of medicine
they'd be always ailing and giving a world
of trouble, and partly because it spoils their
appetites and comes cheaper than breakfast and
dinner. So, it does them good and us good at the
same time, and that's fair enough I'm sure.'

NICHOLAS NICKLEBY

How should one select a playmate for playground games?

Except on the crown, which was raggedly bald, he had stiff, black hair, standing jaggedly all over it, and growing down hill almost to his broad, blunt nose. It was… so much more like the top of a strongly spiked wall than a head of hair, that the best of players at leap-frog might have declined him, as the most dangerous man in the world to go over.

A TALE OF TWO CITIES, ON JERRY CRUNCHER

Why should children be taught more
than just the value of money?

The very first word he learnt to spell was 'gain',
and the second (when he got into two syllables),
'money'. But for two results, which were not
clearly foreseen perhaps by his watchful parent
in the beginning, his training may be said to have
been unexceptionable. One of these flaws was,
that having been long taught by his father to over-
reach everybody, he had imperceptibly acquired
a love of over-reaching that venerable monitor
himself. The other, that from his early habits of
considering everything as a question of property,
he had gradually come to look, with impatience,
on his parent as a certain amount of personal
estate, which had no right whatever to be going
at large, but ought to be secured in that particular
description of iron safe which is commonly
called a coffin, and banked in the grave.

MARTIN CHUZZLEWIT, ON JONAS CHUZZLEWIT

Work

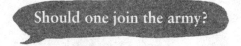

Should one join the army?

The serjeant was describing a military life. It was all drinking, he said, except that there were frequent intervals of eating and love-making.

BARNABY RUDGE

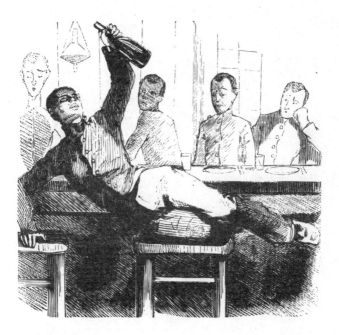

How can one attempt to dissuade one's offspring from a theatrical calling?

'Mr Bazzard's father, being a Norfolk farmer, would have furiously laid about him with a flail, a pitch-fork, and every agricultural implement available for assaulting purposes, on the slightest hint of his son's having written a play.'

THE MYSTERY OF EDWIN DROOD, HIRAM GREWGIOUS

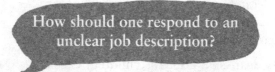

How should one respond to an unclear job description?

'Well,' said that suddenly-transformed individual, as he took his seat on the outside of the Eatanswill coach next morning; 'I wonder whether I'm meant to be a footman, or a groom, or a gamekeeper, or a seedsman. I looks like a sort of compo of every one on 'em. Never mind; there's a change of air, plenty to see, and little to do; and all this suits my complaint uncommon; so long life to the Pickvicks, says I!'

THE PICKWICK PAPERS, SAM WELLER

Why shouldn't an employer eavesdrop on their employees' conversations?

'Mr Scrooge!' said Bob; 'I'll give you Mr Scrooge, the Founder of the Feast!'

'The Founder of the Feast indeed!' cried Mrs Cratchit, reddening. 'I wish I had him here. I'd give him a piece of my mind to feast upon, and I hope he'd have a good appetite for it.'

'My dear,' said Bob, 'the children! Christmas Day.'

'It should be Christmas Day, I am sure,' said she, 'on which one drinks the health of such an odious, stingy, hard, unfeeling man as Mr Scrooge. You know he is, Robert! Nobody knows it better than you do, poor fellow!'

A CHRISTMAS CAROL

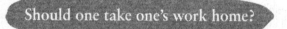

When the diplomatic approach has failed, what is the best way to deal with conflict at work?

For myself, I beg to report that I have my war-paint on, that I have buried the pipe of peace, and am whooping for committee scalps.

LETTER TO MR C. W. DILKE, 19 MARCH 1857

Should one take one's work home?

'No; the office is one thing, and private life is another. When I go into the office, I leave the Castle behind me, and when I come into the Castle, I leave the office behind me.'

GREAT EXPECTATIONS, MR WEMMICK

HOME AND TRAVEL

How important is one's home?

And though home is a name, a word, it is a strong one; stronger than magician ever spoke, or spirit answered to, in strongest conjuration.

MARTIN CHUZZLEWIT

Is an Englishman's home his castle?

'That's a real flagstaff, you see,' said Wemmick, 'and on Sundays I run up a real flag. Then look here. After I have crossed this bridge, I hoist it up-so – and cut off the communication.'

GREAT EXPECTATIONS

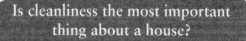

Is cleanliness the most important thing about a house?

Mrs Joe was a very clean housekeeper, but had an exquisite art of making her cleanliness more uncomfortable and unacceptable than the dirt itself.

GREAT EXPECTATIONS

Does a person's environment affect their mood and personality?

His voice is deep and good, his face and figure are good, his manner is a little sombre. His room is a little sombre, and may have had its influence in forming his manner.

THE MYSTERY OF EDWIN DROOD, ON JOHN JASPER

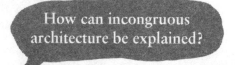

How can incongruous architecture be explained?

They were a gloomy suite of rooms, in a lowering pile of building up a yard, where it had so little business to be, that one could scarcely help fancying it must have run there when it was a young house, playing at hide-and-seek with other houses, and forgotten the way out again.

A CHRISTMAS CAROL

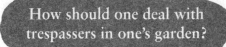

How should one deal with
trespassers in one's garden?

'Let me see you ride a donkey over my
green again, and as sure as you have a
head upon your shoulders, I'll knock
your bonnet off, and tread upon it!'

DAVID COPPERFIELD, BETSEY TROTWOOD

> How may a well-chosen residence
> enable one to indulge one's
> bad habits for free?

Mr Richard Swiveller's apartments were in
the neighbourhood of Drury Lane, and in
addition to this convenience of situation had the
advantage of being over a tobacconist's shop,
so that he was enabled to procure a refreshing
sneeze at any time by merely stepping out
upon the staircase, and was saved the trouble
and expense of maintaining a snuff-box.

THE OLD CURIOSITY SHOP

Where should you go on holiday this year?

'If any one were to ask me what in my opinion was the dullest and most stupid spot on the face of the Earth, I should decidedly say Chelmsford.'

LETTER TO THOMAS BEARD

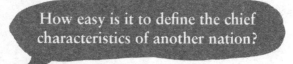

How easy is it to define the chief characteristics of another nation?

All New England is primitive and puritanical. All about and around it is a puddle of mixed human mud, with no such quality in it. Perhaps I may in time sift out some tolerably intelligible whole, but I certainly have not done so yet. It is a good sign, may be, that it all seems immensely more difficult to understand than it was when I was here before.

LETTER TO MISS HOGARTH, 4 JANUARY 1868

How may one recognise that a fellow traveller is best left to himself?

Thus they regarded each other
for some time, in silence.

'Humph!' he said when he had scanned
his features; 'I don't know you.'

'Don't desire to?' – returned the other,
muffling himself as before.

'I don't,' said Gabriel; 'to be plain with
you, friend, you don't carry in your
countenance a letter of recommendation.'

'It's not my wish,' said the traveller.
'My humour is to be avoided.'

'Well,' said the locksmith bluntly, 'I
think you'll have your humour.'

'I will, at any cost,' rejoined the traveller. 'In proof
of it, lay this to heart – that you were never in
such peril of your life as you have been within
these few moments; when you are within five
minutes of breathing your last, you will not be
nearer death than you have been to-night!'

'Aye!' said the sturdy locksmith.

'Aye! and a violent death.'

'From whose hand?'

'From mine,' replied the traveller.

BARNABY RUDGE

How may one detect that one has reached a seaside town, with one's eyes closed?

The air among the houses was of so strong a piscatory flavour that one might have supposed sick fish went up to be dipped in it, as sick people went down to be dipped in the sea.

A TALE OF TWO CITIES

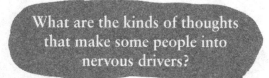

What are the kinds of thoughts that make some people into nervous drivers?

Don't laugh. I am going (alone) in a gig; and, to quote the eloquent inducement which the proprietors of Hampstead *chays* hold out to Sunday riders, 'the gen'l'm'n drives himself.' I am going into Essex and Suffolk. It strikes me I shall be spilt before I pay a turnpike. I have a presentiment I shall run over an only child before I reach Chelmsford, my first stage.

LETTER TO HENRY AUSTIN, 1833/4

PRACTICAL ADVICE FOR
SOCIAL SITUATIONS

How important is it to maintain outward calm during a boring speech?

I dined with Ferguson at the Lord Mayor's, last Tuesday, and had a grimly distracted impulse upon me to defy the toast-master and rush into a speech about him and his noble art, when I sat pining under the imbecility of constitutional and corporational idiots. I did seize him for a moment by the hair of his head (in proposing the Lady Mayoress), and derived some faint consolation from the company's response to the reference. O! no man will ever know under what provocation to contradiction and a savage yell of repudiation I suffered at the hands of ——, feebly complacent in the uniform of Madame Tussaud's own military waxers, and almost the worst speaker I ever heard in my life! Mary and Georgina, sitting on either side of me, urged me to 'look pleasant.' I replied in expressions not to be repeated.

LETTER TO WILLIAM CHARLES KENT, 18 JANUARY 1866

How do you delicately explain table manners to a less refined friend?

'True,' he replied. 'I'll redeem it at once. Let me introduce the topic, Handel, by mentioning that in London it is not the custom to put the knife in the mouth – for fear of accidents – and that while the fork is reserved for that use, it is not put further in than necessary. It is scarcely worth mentioning, only it's as well to do as other people do. Also, the spoon is not generally used over-hand, but under. This has two advantages. You get at your mouth better (which after all is the object), and you save a good deal of the attitude of opening oysters, on the part of the right elbow.'

GREAT EXPECTATIONS, HERBERT POCKET

What is the most unnerving compliment it is possible to give to a man?

'Ah!' said Mrs Gamp, walking away from the bed, 'he'd make a lovely corpse.'

MARTIN CHUZZLEWIT, SARAH GAMP

How may one gracefully give belated thanks for a gift?

Studying the gorilla last night for the twentieth time, it suddenly came into my head that I had never thanked you for that admirable treatise. This is to bear witness to my blushes and repentance. If you knew how much interest it has awakened in me, and how often it has set me a-thinking, you would consider me a more thankless beast than any gorilla that ever lived. But happily you do *not* know, and I am not going to tell you.

LETTER TO PROFESSOR OWEN, 12 JULY 1865

Are manners important even when dealing with a ghost?

'Who are you?'

'Ask me who I was.'

'Who were you then?' said Scrooge, raising his voice. 'You're particular, for a shade.' He was going to say 'to a shade,' but substituted this, as more appropriate.

'In life I was your partner, Jacob Marley.'

'Can you – can you sit down?' asked Scrooge, looking doubtfully at him.

'I can.'

'Do it, then.'

A CHRISTMAS CAROL

Are some ears so refined that care must be taken not to injure them with incorrect English?

'Mr Jasper was that, Tope?'

'Yes, Mr Dean.'

'He has stayed late.'

'Yes, Mr Dean. I have stayed for him, your Reverence. He has been took a little poorly.'

'Say "taken," Tope – to the Dean,' the younger rook interposes in a low tone with this touch of correction, as who should say: 'You may offer bad grammar to the laity, or the humbler clergy, not to the Dean.'

THE MYSTERY OF EDWIN DROOD,
MR TOPE AND MR CRISPARKLE

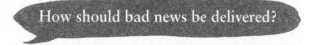

How should bad news be delivered?

'There's no imaginative sentimental humbug about me. I call a spade a spade.'

HARD TIMES, JOSIAH BOUNDERBY

But what if a level of grandeur and theatricality is needed?

Dead, your Majesty. Dead, my lords and gentlemen. Dead, right reverends and wrong reverends of every order. Dead, men and women, born with heavenly compassion in your hearts. And dying thus around us every day.

BLEAK HOUSE

What is the best way to make foreign guests feel uncomfortable in your company?

'This Island was Blest, Sir, to the Direct Exclusion of such Other Countries as – as there may happen to be. And if we were all Englishmen present, I would say,' added Mr Podsnap, looking round upon his compatriots, and sounding solemnly with his theme, 'that there is in the Englishman a combination of qualities, a modesty, an independence, a responsibility, a repose, combined with an absence of everything calculated to call a blush into the cheek of a young person, which one would seek in vain among the Nations of the Earth.'

OUR MUTUAL FRIEND, JOHN PODSNAP

> What is it that leads ladies to visit one
> another in the middle of the afternoon?

It has been said that Mrs Quilp was pining in her
bower. In her bower she was, but not alone, for
besides the old lady her mother of whom mention
has recently been made, there were present some
half-dozen ladies of the neighborhood who had
happened by a strange accident (and also by a
little understanding among themselves) to drop in
one after another, just about tea-time. This being
a season favourable to conversation, and the
room being a cool, shady, lazy kind of place, with
some plants at the open window shutting out the
dust, and interposing pleasantly enough between
the tea table within and the old Tower without,
it is no wonder that the ladies felt an inclination
to talk and linger, especially when there are taken
into account the additional inducements of fresh
butter, new bread, shrimps, and watercresses.

THE OLD CURIOSITY SHOP

What sentiments should not be
included in Christmas cards?

'Merry Christmas! Out upon merry Christmas!
What's Christmas time to you but a time for
paying bills without money; a time for finding
yourself a year older, but not an hour richer;
a time for balancing your books and having
every item in 'em through a round dozen
of months presented dead against you? If I
could work my will,' said Scrooge indignantly,
'every idiot who goes about with "Merry
Christmas" on his lips, should be boiled with
his own pudding, and buried with a stake
of holly through his heart. He should!'

A CHRISTMAS CAROL

How should you deal with door-to-door charity collectors?

'What shall I put you down for?'

'Nothing!' Scrooge replied.

'You wish to be anonymous?'

'I wish to be left alone,' said Scrooge. 'Since you ask me what I wish, gentlemen, that is my answer. I don't make merry myself at Christmas and I can't afford to make idle people merry. I help to support the establishments I have mentioned – they cost enough; and those who are badly off must go there.'

'Many can't go there; and many would rather die.'

'If they would rather die,' said Scrooge, 'they had better do it, and decrease the surplus population. Besides – excuse me – I don't know that.'

'But you might know it,' observed the gentleman.

'It's not my business,' Scrooge returned. 'It's enough for a man to understand his own business, and not to interfere with other people's. Mine occupies me constantly. Good afternoon, gentlemen!'

A CHRISTMAS CAROL

> When is the best time of day
> for people-watching?

Night is generally my time for walking. In
the summer I often leave home early in the
morning, and roam about fields and lanes all
day, or even escape for days or weeks together;
but, saving in the country, I seldom go out until
after dark, though, Heaven be thanked, I love
its light and feel the cheerfulness it sheds upon
the earth, as much as any creature living.

I have fallen insensibly into this habit, both
because it favours my infirmity and because it
affords me greater opportunity of speculating on
the characters and occupations of those who fill
the streets. The glare and hurry of broad noon are
not adapted to idle pursuits like mine; a glimpse
of passing faces caught by the light of a street-
lamp or a shop window is often better for my
purpose than their full revelation in the daylight;
and, if I must add the truth, night is kinder in
this respect than day, which too often destroys an
air-built castle at the moment of its completion,
without the least ceremony or remorse.

THE OLD CURIOSITY SHOP

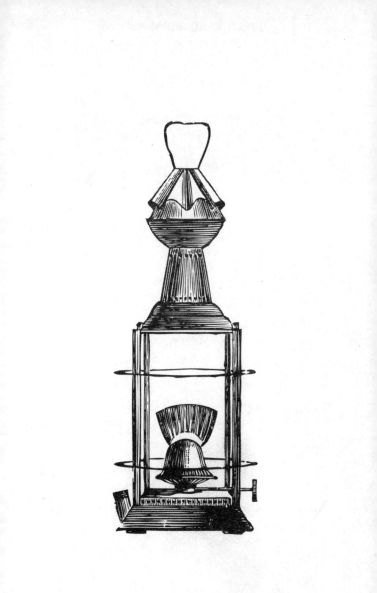

> What is the best way to stay safe in the midst of a mob?

'Slumkey for ever!' roared the honest and independent.

'Slumkey for ever!' echoed Mr Pickwick, taking off his hat. 'No Fizkin!' roared the crowd.

'Certainly not!' shouted Mr Pickwick. 'Hurrah!' And then there was another roaring, like that of a whole menagerie when the elephant has rung the bell for the cold meat.

'Who is Slumkey?' whispered Mr Tupman.

'I don't know,' replied Mr Pickwick, in the same tone. 'Hush. Don't ask any questions. It's always best on these occasions to do what the mob do.'

'But suppose there are two mobs?' suggested Mr Snodgrass.

'Shout with the largest,' replied Mr Pickwick.

THE PICKWICK PAPERS

PASTIMES AND CELEBRATIONS

> What benefits does playing
> an instrument have on
> attracting a suitor?

Once, when there was a pause in the dancing,
Lady Skettles told Paul that he seemed very fond
of music. Paul replied, that he was; and if she was
too, she ought to hear his sister, Florence, sing.
Lady Skettles presently discovered that she was
dying with anxiety to have that gratification; and
though Florence was at first very much frightened
at being asked to sing before so many people,
and begged earnestly to be excused, yet, on Paul
calling her to him, and saying, 'Do, Floy! Please!
For me, my dear!' she went straight to the piano,
and began. When they all drew a little away, that
Paul might see her; and when he saw her sitting
there all alone, so young, and good, and beautiful,
and kind to him; and heard her thrilling voice,
so natural and sweet, and such a golden link
between him and all his life's love and happiness,
rising out of the silence; he turned his face away,
and hid his tears. Not, as he told them when they
spoke to him, not that the music was too plaintive
or too sorrowful, but it was so dear to him.

DOMBEY AND SON

What is the best way to provide piano accompaniment for a wayward singer?

It was a consequence of his playing the accompaniment without notes, and of her being a heedless little creature, very apt to go wrong, that he followed her lips most attentively, with his eyes as well as hands; carefully and softly hinting the key-note from time to time.

THE MYSTERY OF EDWIN DROOD

How may one describe the delights
of a wax-work collection?

'It's calm and – what's that word again –
critical? – no – classical, that's it – it's calm and
classical. No low beatings and knockings about,
no jokings and squeakings like your precious
Punches, but always the same, with a constantly
unchanging air of coldness and gentility; and
so like life, that if wax-work only spoke and
walked about, you'd hardly know the difference.
I won't go so far as to say, that, as it is, I've seen
wax-work quite like life, but I've certainly seen
some life that was exactly like wax-work.'

THE OLD CURIOSITY SHOP, MRS JARLEY

How may one encourage
an amateur boxer to keep
up his training?

'I say, every morning of my life, that
you'll do it at last, Sept,' remarked the old
lady, looking on; 'and so you will.'

'Do what, Ma dear?'

'Break the pier-glass, or burst a blood-vessel.'

THE MYSTERY OF EDWIN DROOD, MRS CRISPARKLE
AND THE REVEREND SEPTIMUS CRISPARKLE

How should one celebrate being
extricated from a chimney?

'Bring in the bottled lightning, a
clean tumbler, and a corkscrew.'

NICHOLAS NICKLEBY, THE OLD GENTLEMAN
WHO GETS CAUGHT IN THE CHIMNEY

Can one worship at the altars of Architecture and Geology simultaneously?

'People objected to Professor Dingo when we were staying in the north of Devon after our marriage,' said Mrs Badger, 'that he disfigured some of the houses and other buildings by chipping off fragments of those edifices with his little geological hammer. But the professor replied that he knew of no building save the Temple of Science.'

BLEAK HOUSE

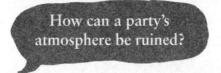

How can a party's
atmosphere be ruined?

The apparition of a file of soldiers ringing down
the butt-ends of their loaded muskets on our
door-step, caused the dinner-party to rise from
table in confusion, and caused Mrs Joe re-entering
the kitchen empty-handed, to stop short and stare,
in her wondering lament of 'Gracious goodness
gracious me, what's gone – with the – pie!'

GREAT EXPECTATIONS

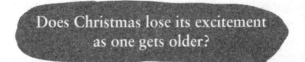

Does Christmas lose its excitement
as one gets older?

'I don't know what to do!' cried Scrooge,
laughing and crying in the same breath; and
making a perfect Laocoön of himself with his
stockings. 'I am as light as a feather, I am as
happy as an angel, I am as merry as a schoolboy.
I am as giddy as a drunken man. A merry
Christmas to everybody! A happy New Year
to all the world. Hallo here! Whoop! Hallo!'

A CHRISTMAS CAROL

Is it always comfortable to be a little boy at a Christmas feast?

Among this good company I should have felt myself, even if I hadn't robbed the pantry, in a false position. Not because I was squeezed in at an acute angle of the tablecloth, with the table in my chest, and the Pumblechookian elbow in my eye, nor because I was not allowed to speak (I didn't want to speak), nor because I was regaled with the scaly tips of the drumsticks of the fowls, and with those obscure corners of pork of which the pig, when living, had had the least reason to be vain. No; I should not have minded that, if they would only have left me alone. But they wouldn't leave me alone. They seemed to think the opportunity lost, if they failed to point the conversation at me, every now and then, and stick the point into me.

GREAT EXPECTATIONS

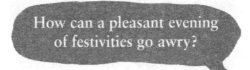

How can a pleasant evening of festivities go awry?

Somebody was leaning out of my bedroom window, refreshing his forehead against the cool stone of the parapet, and feeling the air upon his face. It was myself. I was addressing myself as 'Copperfield', and saying, 'Why did you try to smoke? You might have known you couldn't do it.' Now, somebody was unsteadily contemplating his features in the looking-glass. That was I too. I was very pale in the looking-glass; my eyes had a vacant appearance; and my hair – only my hair, nothing else – looked drunk.

DAVID COPPERFIELD

> Can anything be used
> as a reason to drink?

The horse, whose health had been
drunk in his absence, was standing
outside: ready harnessed to the cart.

OLIVER TWIST

> What is the appropriate time to
> declare a party finished?

'… about one o'clock in the morning, the
bailie's grown-up son became insensible while
attempting the first verse of "Willie brewed a
peck o' maut"; and he having been, for half an
hour before, the only other man visible above
the mahogany, it occurred to my uncle that it
was almost time to think about going, especially
as drinking had set in at seven o'clock, in order
that he might get home at a decent hour.'

THE PICKWICK PAPERS, THE BAGMAN

FASHION AND BEAUTY

How can a lady swiftly pep up her appearance at a social gathering?

'The word Papa, besides, gives a pretty form to the lips. Papa, potatoes, poultry, prunes, and prism are all very good words for the lips: especially prunes and prism. You will find it serviceable, in the formation of a demeanour, if you sometimes say to yourself in company – on entering a room, for instance – Papa, potatoes, poultry, prunes and prism, prunes and prism.'

LITTLE DORRIT, MRS GENERAL

How important is it to dress well for a journey?

Mr Pickwick proceeded to put himself into his clothes, and his clothes into his portmanteau. Great men are seldom over scrupulous in the arrangement of their attire; the operation of shaving, dressing, and coffee-imbibing was soon performed; and, in another hour, Mr Pickwick, with his portmanteau in his hand, his telescope in his greatcoat pocket, and his note-book in his waistcoat, ready for the reception of any discoveries worthy of being noted down, had arrived at the coach-stand in St Martin's-le-Grand. 'Cab!' said Mr Pickwick.

THE PICKWICK PAPERS

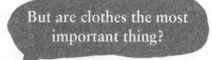

But are clothes the most important thing?

'Any man may be in good spirits and good temper when he's well dressed. There ain't much credit in that. If I was very ragged and very jolly, then I should begin to feel I had gained a point, Mr Pinch.'

MARTIN CHUZZLEWIT, MARK TAPLEY

Is it more important to be elegant, or simply to be at ease with one's appearance?

To say that she had two left legs, and somebody else's arms, and that all four limbs seemed to be out of joint, and to start from perfectly wrong places when they were set in motion, is to offer the mildest outline of the reality. To say that she was perfectly content and satisfied with these arrangements, and regarded them as being no business of hers, and that she took her arms and legs as they came, and allowed them to dispose of themselves just as it happened, is to render faint justice to her equanimity. Her dress was a prodigious pair of self-willed shoes, that never wanted to go where her feet went; blue stockings; a printed gown of many colours, and the most hideous pattern procurable for money; and a white apron. She always wore short sleeves, and always had, by some accident, grazed elbows, in which she took so lively an interest, that she was continually trying to turn them round and get impossible views of them. In general, a little cap placed somewhere on her head; though it was rarely to be met with in the place usually occupied in other subjects, by that article of dress; but, from head to foot she was scrupulously clean, and maintained a kind of dislocated tidiness.

THE BATTLE OF LIFE, ON CLEMENCY NEWCOME

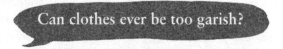

Can clothes ever be too garish?

His wardrobe was extensive – very extensive
– not strictly classical perhaps, not quite new,
nor did it contain any one garment made
precisely after the fashion of any age or time,
but everything was more or less spangled;
and what can be prettier than spangles!

THE PICKWICK PAPERS, ON MR SOLOMON LUCAS

Surely there's no harm in showing ourselves to our best advantage?

If there were no such thing as display in the world, my private opinion is, and I hope you agree with me, that we might get on a great deal better than we do, and might be infinitely more agreeable company than we are.

THE BATTLE OF LIFE

What influence does one's workwear wield on the gentler sex?

'We know, Mr Weller – we, who are men of the world – that a good uniform must work its way with the women, sooner or later. In fact, that's the only thing, between you and me, that makes the service worth entering into.'

THE PICKWICK PAPERS, A FOOTMAN

How may one's children assist in the adjustment of one's coiffure?

'Now, you may give me a kiss, Pa, and I should like to give your hair a turn, because it has been dreadfully neglected in my absence.'

R. W. submitted his head to the operator, and the operator went on talking; at the same time putting separate locks of his hair through a curious process of being smartly rolled over her two revolving forefingers, which were then suddenly pulled out of it in opposite lateral directions. On each of these occasions the patient winced and winked.

OUR MUTUAL FRIEND, BELLA WILFER AND HER FATHER

FOOD AND DRINK

What is more real: indigestion or the supernatural?

'You don't believe in me,' observed the Ghost.

'I don't,' said Scrooge.

'What evidence would you have of my reality beyond that of your senses?'

'I don't know,' said Scrooge.

'Why do you doubt your senses?'

'Because,' said Scrooge, 'a little thing affects them. A slight disorder of the stomach makes them cheats. You may be an undigested bit of beef, a blot of mustard, a crumb of cheese, a fragment of an underdone potato. There's more of gravy than of grave about you, whatever you are!'

A Christmas Carol

What is an appropriately patriotic toast, to be used in the presence of visitors?

'When the French come over,
May we meet them at Dover!'

THE MYSTERY OF EDWIN DROOD, MR SAPSEA

How can one avoid drinking too much?

'And whatever you do, young woman, don't bring more than a shilling's-worth of gin and water-warm when I rings the bell a second time; for that is always my allowance, and I never takes a drop beyond!'

MARTIN CHUZZLWIT, SARAH GAMP

What is the best and most direct way to ask for a second helping of dinner?

'Please, sir, I want some more.'

OLIVER TWIST, Oliver Twist

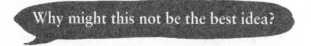

Why might this not be the best idea?

'Mr Limbkins, I beg your pardon, sir! Oliver Twist has asked for more!'

There was a general start. Horror was depicted on every countenance.

'For more!' said Mr Limbkins. 'Compose yourself, Bumble, and answer me distinctly. Do I understand that he asked for more, after he had eaten the supper allotted by the dietary?'

'He did, sir,' replied Bumble.

'That boy will be hung,' said the gentleman in the white waistcoat. 'I know that boy will be hung.'

Nobody controverted the prophetic gentleman's opinion.

OLIVER TWIST

What impression does eating too quickly give of a person?

He was already handing mincemeat down his throat in the most curious manner – more like a man who was putting it away somewhere in a violent hurry, than a man who was eating it – but he left off to take some of the liquor.

GREAT EXPECTATIONS, ON ABEL MAGWITCH

How may one sustain oneself through a lengthy theatre tour?

A dozen oysters and a little champagne between the parts every night, constitute the best restorative I have ever yet tried.

LETTER TO MISS MAMIE DICKENS, 14 APRIL 1866

How can rhetoric gain
you a free meal?

'My dear Jarndyce,' he returned, 'you surprise
me. You take the butcher's position. A butcher I
once dealt with occupied that very ground. Says
he, "Sir, why did you eat spring lamb at eighteen
pence a pound?" "Why did I eat spring lamb
at eighteen pence a pound, my honest friend?"
said I, naturally amazed by the question. "I like
spring lamb!" This was so far convincing. "Well,
sir," says he, "I wish I had meant the lamb as
you mean the money!" "My good fellow," said
I, "pray let us reason like intellectual beings.
How could that be? It was impossible. You HAD
got the lamb, and I have NOT got the money.
You couldn't really mean the lamb without
sending it in, whereas I can, and do, really
mean the money without paying it!" He had
not a word. There was an end of the subject.'

BLEAK HOUSE, HAROLD SKIMPOLE

MONEY

What is the secret to happiness?

'Annual income twenty pounds, annual expenditure nineteen nineteen and six, result happiness. Annual income twenty pounds, annual expenditure twenty pounds ought and six, result misery.'

DAVID COPPERFIELD, WILKINS MICAWBER

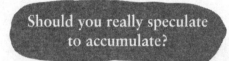

Should you really speculate to accumulate?

Speculation is a round game; the players see little or nothing of their cards at first starting; gains MAY be great – and so may losses. The run of luck went against Mr Nickleby. A mania prevailed, a bubble burst, four stock-brokers took villa residences at Florence, four hundred nobodies were ruined, and among them Mr Nickleby.

NICHOLAS NICKLEBY

Is it true that a life of bill-avoidance
limits one's horizons somewhat?

'I enter in this little book the names of the streets
that I can't go down while the shops are open.
This dinner today closes Long Acre. I bought a
pair of boots in Great Queen Street last week,
and made that no throughfare too. There's only
one avenue to the Strand left often now, and I
shall have to stop up that to-night with a pair
of gloves. The roads are closing so fast in every
direction, that in a month's time, unless my aunt
sends me a remittance, I shall have to go three
or four miles out of town to get over the way.'

THE OLD CURIOSITY SHOP, DICK SWIVELLER

> To what extremes will poverty drive people?

A large cask of wine had been dropped and broken, in the street. The accident had happened in getting it out of a cart; the cask had tumbled out with a run, the hoops had burst, and it lay on the stones just outside the door of the wine-shop, shattered like a walnut-shell.

All the people within reach had suspended their business, or their idleness, to run to the spot and drink the wine. The rough, irregular stones of the street, pointing every way, and designed, one might have thought, expressly to lame all living creatures that approached them, had dammed it into little pools; these were surrounded, each by its own jostling group or crowd, according to its size. Some men kneeled down, made scoops of their two hands joined, and sipped, or tried to help women, who bent over their shoulders, to sip, before the wine had all run out between their fingers.

A TALE OF TWO CITIES

What are the secret tragedies and hopes of a life lived in poverty?

So poor a clerk, though having a limited salary and an unlimited family, that he had never yet attained the modest object of his ambition: which was, to wear a complete new suit of clothes, hat and boots included, at one time. His black hat was brown before he could afford a coat, his pantaloons were white at the seams and knees before he could buy a pair of boots, his boots had worn out before he could treat himself to new pantaloons, and, by the time he worked round to the hat again, that shining modern article roofed-in an ancient ruin of various periods.

OUR MUTUAL FRIEND, ON REGINALD WILFER

Does a man have room in his
life for unlimited passions?

'It matters little,' she said, softly. 'To you,
very little. Another idol has displaced
me; and if it can cheer and comfort you
in time to come, as I would have tried to
do, I have no just cause to grieve.'

'What idol has displaced you?' he rejoined.

'A golden one.'

A CHRISTMAS CAROL, EBENEZER SCROOGE
AND THE GHOST OF CHRISTMAS PAST

THE DARKER
SIDE OF MAN

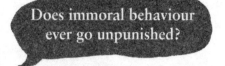

Does immoral behaviour ever go unpunished?

'It may be profitable to you to reflect, in future, that there never were greed and cunning in the world yet, that did not do too much, and over-reach themselves. It is as certain as death.'

DAVID COPPERFIELD, DAVID COPPERFIELD

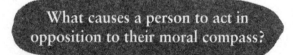

What causes a person to act in opposition to their moral compass?

In a word, I was too cowardly to do what I knew to be right, as I had been too cowardly to avoid doing what I knew to be wrong.

GREAT EXPECTATIONS

Is it true that a person can be their own worst enemy?

'Every man's his own friend, my dear,' replied Fagin, with his most insinuating grin. 'He hasn't as good a one as himself anywhere.'

'Except sometimes,' replied Morris Bolter, assuming the air of a man of the world. 'Some people are nobody's enemies but their own, yer know.'

OLIVER TWIST

How can nothing occurring be as frightening as something occurring?

Now, being prepared for almost anything, he was not by any means prepared for nothing; and, consequently, when the bell struck one, and no shape appeared, he was taken with a violent fit of trembling. Five minutes, ten minutes, a quarter of an hour went by, yet nothing came.

A CHRISTMAS CAROL, ON EBENEZER SCROOGE

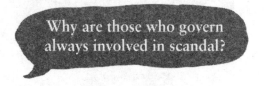

Why are those who govern always involved in scandal?

It is an old prerogative of kings to govern everything but their passions.

THE PICKWICK PAPERS

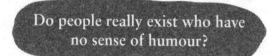

Do people really exist who have
no sense of humour?

'Hah! I expected to see you older, sir.'

'I hope you will,' was the good-humoured reply.

'Eh?' demanded Mr Honeythunder.

'Only a poor little joke. Not worth repeating.'

'Joke? Ay; I never see a joke,' Mr
Honeythunder frowningly retorted. 'A
joke is wasted upon me, sir.'

THE MYSTERY OF EDWIN DROOD, MR HONEYTHUNDER
AND THE REVEREND SEPTIMUS CRISPARKLE

What effect can incarceration have on a person's mind?

'Five paces by four and a half, five paces by four and a half, five paces by four and a half.' The prisoner walked to and fro in his cell, counting its measurement, and the roar of the city arose like muffled drums with a wild swell of voices added to them. 'He made shoes, he made shoes, he made shoes.' The prisoner counted the measurement again, and paced faster, to draw his mind with him from that latter repetition. 'The ghosts that vanished when the wicket closed. There was one among them, the appearance of a lady dressed in black, who was leaning in the embrasure of a window, and she had a light shining upon her golden hair, and she looked like * * * * Let us ride on again, for God's sake, through the illuminated villages with the people all awake! * * * * He made shoes, he made shoes, he made shoes. * * * * Five paces by four and a half.'

A TALE OF TWO CITIES, CHARLES DARNAY

Should a condemned man conduct
to the scaffold in thoughtful silence?

The Ordinary coming up at this moment,
reproved him for his indecent mirth, and
advised him to alter his demeanour.

'And why, master?' said Hugh. 'Can I do better
than bear it easily? YOU bear it easily enough.
Oh! never tell me,' he cried, as the other would
have spoken, 'for all your sad look and your
solemn air, you think little enough of it! They
say you're the best maker of lobster salads in
London. Ha, ha! I've heard that, you see, before
now. Is it a good one, this morning – is your hand
in? How does the breakfast look? I hope there's
enough, and to spare, for all this hungry company
that'll sit down to it, when the sight's over.'

BARNABY RUDGE

Are there benefits to being called a madman?

It's a fine name. Show me the monarch whose angry frown was ever feared like the glare of a madman's eye – whose cord and axe were ever half so sure as a madman's gripe.

THE PICKWICK PAPERS

How fickle are the general public?

At every vote (the Jurymen voted aloud and individually), the populace set up a shout of applause. All the voices were in the prisoner's favour, and the President declared him free.

Then, began one of those extraordinary scenes with which the populace sometimes gratified their fickleness, or their better impulses towards generosity and mercy, or which they regarded as some set-off against their swollen account of cruel rage. No man can decide now to which of these motives such extraordinary scenes were referable; it is probable, to a blending of all the three, with the second predominating. No sooner was the acquittal pronounced, than tears were shed as freely as blood at another time, and such fraternal embraces were bestowed upon the prisoner by as many of both sexes as could rush at him, that after his long and unwholesome confinement he was in danger of fainting from exhaustion; none the less because he knew very well, that the very same people, carried by another current, would have rushed at him with the very same intensity, to rend him to pieces and strew him over the streets.

A TALE OF TWO CITIES

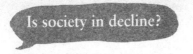

Is society in decline?

It is a pleasant thing to reflect upon, and furnishes a complete answer to those who contend for the gradual degeneration of the human species, that every baby born into the world is a finer one than the last.

Nicholas Nickleby

And what about America?

Martin knew nothing about America, or he would have known perfectly well that if its individual citizens, to a man, are to be believed, it always IS depressed, and always IS stagnated, and always IS at an alarming crisis, and never was otherwise; though as a body they are ready to make oath upon the Evangelists at any hour of the day or night, that it is the most thriving and prosperous of all countries on the habitable globe.

Martin Chuzzlewit

> What is the difference between animals and humans?

He was the meanest cur existing, with a single pair of legs. And instinct (a word we all clearly understand) going largely on four legs, and reason always on two, meanness on four legs never attains the perfection of meanness on two.

OUR MUTUAL FRIEND

> How powerful can symbols of death be?

It was the popular theme for jests; it was the best cure for headache, it infallibly prevented the hair from turning grey, it imparted a peculiar delicacy to the complexion, it was the National Razor which shaved close: who kissed La Guillotine, looked through the little window and sneezed into the sack. It was the sign of the regeneration of the human race. It superseded the Cross. Models of it were worn on breasts from which the Cross was discarded, and it was bowed down to and believed in where the Cross was denied.

A TALE OF TWO CITIES

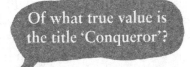

Of what true value is the title 'Conqueror'?

The moment he was dead, his physicians, priests, and nobles, not knowing what contest for the throne might now take place, or what might happen in it, hastened away, each man for himself and his own property; the mercenary servants of the court began to rob and plunder; the body of the King, in the indecent strife, was rolled from the bed, and lay alone, for hours, upon the ground. O Conqueror, of whom so many great names are proud now, of whom so many great names thought nothing then, it were better to have conquered one true heart, than England!

A CHILD'S HISTORY OF ENGLAND

HEALTH AND INFIRMITY

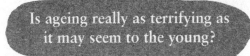

Is ageing really as terrifying as
it may seem to the young?

But they were scarcely less beautiful in their
slow decline, than they had been in their prime;
for nature gives to every time and season some
beauties of its own; and from morning to
night, as from the cradle to the grave, is but
a succession of changes so gentle and easy,
that we can scarcely mark their progress.

NICHOLAS NICKLEBY

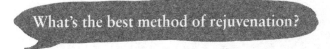

What's the best method of rejuvenation?

When this result was brought about, old
Fezziwig, clapping his hands to stop the dance,
cried out, 'Well done!' and the fiddler plunged
his hot face into a pot of porter, especially
provided for that purpose. But scorning rest,
upon his reappearance, he instantly began again,
though there were no dancers yet, as if the
other fiddler had been carried home, exhausted,
on a shutter, and he were a brand-new man
resolved to beat him out of sight, or perish.

A CHRISTMAS CAROL

What's the best way to
treat a bruised eye?

'Sir? Waiter! Raw beef-steak for the gentleman's
eye – nothing like raw beef-steak for a bruise,
sir; cold lamp-post very good, but lamp-post
inconvenient – damned odd standing in the
open street half an hour, with your eye against
a lamp-post – eh, – very good – ha! ha!'

THE PICKWICK PAPERS, ALFRED JINGLE

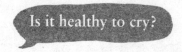

Is it healthy to cry?

'It opens the lungs, washes the countenance, exercises the eyes, and softens down the temper,' said Mr Bumble. 'So cry away.'

OLIVER TWIST

But is it acceptable to do so?

Heaven knows we need never be ashamed of our tears, for they are rain upon the blinding dust of earth, overlying our hard hearts.

GREAT EXPECTATIONS

What is the attraction of moping?

This consolatory farewell, Mrs Wickam accompanied with a look of heartfelt anguish; and being left alone with the two children again, and becoming conscious that the wind was blowing mournfully, she indulged in melancholy – that cheapest and most accessible of luxuries – until she was overpowered by slumber.

DOMBEY AND SON

How important in life is the idea of moderation?

'… vices are sometimes only virtues carried to excess!'

DOMBEY AND SON, MR MORFIN

Why should you always be aware of your surroundings?

'Heads, heads – take care of your heads!' cried the loquacious stranger, as they came out under the low archway, which in those days formed the entrance to the coach-yard. 'Terrible place – dangerous work – other day – five children – mother – tall lady, eating sandwiches – forgot the arch – crash – knock – children look round – mother's head off – sandwich in her hand – no mouth to put it in – head of a family off – shocking, shocking! Looking at Whitehall, sir? – fine place – little window – somebody else's head off there, eh, sir? – he didn't keep a sharp look-out enough either – eh, Sir, eh?'

THE PICKWICK PAPERS, ALFRED JINGLE

What is the best way to become refreshed?

'There's nothin' so refreshen' as sleep, sir, as the servant girl said afore she drank the egg-cupful of laudanum.'

THE PICKWICK PAPERS, SAM WELLER

Is medicine always to be trusted?

'Some medical beast had revived tar-water in those days as a fine medicine, and Mrs Joe always kept a supply of it in the cupboard; having a belief in its virtues correspondent to its nastiness. At the best of times, so much of this elixir was administered to me as a choice restorative, that I was conscious of going about, smelling like a new fence.'

GREAT EXPECTATIONS, PIP PIRRIP

What effect can an easy life have on a person's intellect?

… certain it is that minds, like bodies, will often fall into a pimpled ill-conditioned state from mere excess of comfort, and like them, are often successfully cured by remedies in themselves very nauseous and unpalatable.

BARNABY RUDGE

Is there any benefit to having an opium addiction?

'O my poor head! I makes my pipes of old penny ink-bottles, ye see, deary – this is one – and I fits-in a mouthpiece, this way, and I takes my mixter out of this thimble with this little horn spoon; and so I fills, deary. Ah, my poor nerves! I got Heavens-hard drunk for sixteen year afore I took to this; but this don't hurt me, not to speak of. And it takes away the hunger as well as wittles, deary.'

THE MYSTERY OF EDWIN DROOD, WOMAN IN THE OPIUM DEN

What are the causes of madness?

The thoughtless riot, dissipation, and debauchery of his younger days produced fever and delirium. The first effects of the latter was the strange delusion, founded upon a well-known medical theory, strongly contended for by some, and as strongly contested by others, that an hereditary madness existed in his family. This produced a settled gloom, which in time developed a morbid insanity, and finally terminated in raving madness.

THE PICKWICK PAPERS

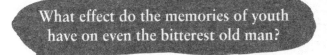

What effect do the memories of youth have on even the bitterest old man?

The jocund travellers came on; and as they came, Scrooge knew and named them every one. Why was he rejoiced beyond all bounds to see them! Why did his cold eye glisten, and his heart leap up as they went past! Why was he filled with gladness when he heard them give each other Merry Christmas, as they parted at cross-roads and bye-ways, for their several homes!

A CHRISTMAS CAROL

What is one early indication that somebody nearby may have... spontaneously combusted?

'Why, I have noticed myself that there is a queer kind of flavour in the place to-night,' Mr Weevle rejoins. 'I suppose it's chops at the Sol's Arms.'

'Chops, do you think? Oh! Chops, eh?' Mr Snagsby sniffs and tastes again. 'Well, sir, I suppose it is. But I should say their cook at the Sol wanted a little looking after. She has been burning 'em, sir! And I don't think' – Mr Snagsby sniffs and tastes again and then spits and wipes his mouth – 'I don't think – not to put too fine a point upon it – that they were quite fresh when they were shown the gridiron.'

BLEAK HOUSE

> What is the best course of treatment
> when one has fallen through
> the ice while skating?

Mr Pickwick paused not an instant until he was snug in bed. Sam Weller lighted a blazing fire in the room, and took up his dinner; a bowl of punch was carried up afterwards, and a grand carouse held in honour of his safety. Old Wardle would not hear of his rising, so they made the bed the chair, and Mr Pickwick presided. A second and a third bowl were ordered in; and when Mr Pickwick awoke next morning, there was not a symptom of rheumatism about him; which proves, as Mr Bob Sawyer very justly observed, that there is nothing like hot punch in such cases; and that if ever hot punch did fail to act as a preventive, it was merely because the patient fell into the vulgar error of not taking enough of it.

THE PICKWICK PAPERS

THE WRITTEN WORD

Are there always enough words in the dictionary, or is it sometimes necessary to coin new terms?

'There will be a world more wiglomeration about it, I suppose, but it must be done.'

'More what, guardian?' said I.

'More wiglomeration,' said he. 'It's the only name I know for the thing. He is a ward in Chancery, my dear. Kenge and Carboy will have something to say about it; Master Somebody – a sort of ridiculous sexton, digging graves for the merits of causes in a back room at the end of Quality Court, Chancery Lane – will have something to say about it; counsel will have something to say about it; the Chancellor will have something to say about it; the satellites will have something to say about it; they will all have to be handsomely fee'd, all round, about it; the whole thing will be vastly ceremonious, wordy, unsatisfactory, and expensive, and I call it, in general, wiglomeration. How mankind ever came to be afflicted with wiglomeration, or for whose sins these young people ever fell into a pit of it, I don't know; so it is.'

BLEAK HOUSE, MR JARNDYCE AND ESTHER SUMMERSON

Should you judge a book by its cover?

'There are books of which the backs and covers are by far the best parts.'

OLIVER TWIST, MR BROWNLOW

How should a writer portray the actions of their characters most effectively?

… it strikes me that you constantly hurry your narrative (and yet without getting on) *by telling it, in a sort of impetuous breathless way, in your own person, when the people should tell it and act it for themselves.* My notion always is, that when I have made the people to play out the play, it is, as it were, their business to do it, and not mine.

LETTER TO MRS BROOKFIELD, 20 FEBRUARY 1866

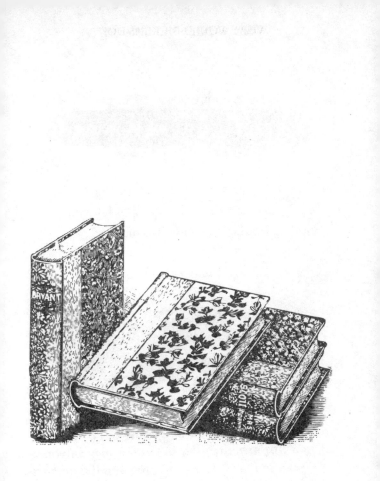

Does writing about sad
events help or hinder?

It is no worse, because I write of it. It would
be no better, if I stopped my most unwilling
hand. It is done. Nothing can undo it; nothing
can make it otherwise than as it was.

DAVID COPPERFIELD

Need one worry too much about
the sensibilities of foreign readers,
when writing of their nations?

As I had never, in writing fiction, had any
disposition to soften what is ridiculous or wrong
at home, so I then hoped that the good-humoured
people of the United States would not be generally
disposed to quarrel with me for carrying the same
usage abroad. I am happy to believe that my
confidence in that great nation was not misplaced.

MARTIN CHUZZLEWIT, PREFACE

How should you go about convincing an acquaintance to contribute to your publication?

When are you going to send something more to H. W.? Are you lazy?? Low-spirited??? Pining for Paris????

LETTER TO REV JAMES WHITE, 8 FEBRUARY 1857

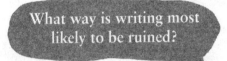

What way is writing most likely to be ruined?

These 'Notes' are destroyed by too much smartness. It gives the appearance of perpetual effort, stabs to the heart the nature that is in them, and wearies by the manner and not by the matter. It is the commonest fault in the world (as I have constant occasion to observe here), but it is a very great one... Again I must say, above all things – especially to young people writing: For the love of God don't condescend! Don't assume the attitude of saying, 'See how clever I am, and what fun everybody else is!' Take any shape but that.

LETTER TO MR FRANK STONE, A. R. A., 1 JUNE 1857

> Are books the only source of
> literary inspiration?

'I an't married, Mister,' said Clemency.

'Oh! I beg your pardon. I should think not,'
chuckled Snitchey, casting his eyes over her
extraordinary figure. 'You CAN read?'

'A little,' answered Clemency.

'The marriage service, night and morning,
eh?' observed the lawyer, jocosely.

'No,' said Clemency. 'Too hard.
I only reads a thimble.'

'Read a thimble!' echoed Snitchey. 'What
are you talking about, young woman?'

Clemency nodded. 'And a nutmeg-grater.'

THE BATTLE OF LIFE

Why is it not always best to have
someone read to you?

Miss Twinkleton didn't read fairly. She cut the
love-scenes, interpolated passages in praise of
female celibacy, and was guilty of other glaring
pious frauds. As an instance in point, take the
glowing passage: 'Ever dearest and best adored,
– said Edward, clasping the dear head to his
breast, and drawing the silken hair through
his caressing fingers, from which he suffered it
to fall like golden rain, – ever dearest and best
adored, let us fly from the unsympathetic world
and the sterile coldness of the stony-hearted,
to the rich warm Paradise of Trust and Love.'
Miss Twinkleton's fraudulent version tamely ran
thus: 'Ever engaged to me with the consent of

our parents on both sides, and the approbation of the silver-haired rector of the district, – said Edward, respectfully raising to his lips the taper fingers so skilful in embroidery, tambour, crochet, and other truly feminine arts, – let me call on thy papa ere tomorrow's dawn has sunk into the west, and propose a suburban establishment, lowly it may be, but within our means, where he will be always welcome as an evening guest, and where every arrangement shall invest economy, and constant interchange of scholastic acquirements with the attributes of the ministering angel to domestic bliss.'

THE MYSTERY OF EDWIN DROOD

How do books help a child
cope with difficult times?

My father had left a small collection of books
in a little room upstairs, to which I had access
(for it adjoined my own) and which nobody
else in our house ever troubled. From that
blessed little room, Roderick Random, Peregrine
Pickle, Humphrey Clinker, Tom Jones, the
Vicar of Wakefield, Don Quixote, Gil Blas, and
Robinson Crusoe, came out, a glorious host, to
keep me company. They kept alive my fancy,
and my hope of something beyond that place
and time – they, and the Arabian Nights, and
the Tales of the Genii – and did me no harm;
for whatever harm was in some of them was
not there for me; I knew nothing of it. It is
astonishing to me now, how I found time, in
the midst of my porings and blunderings over
heavier themes, to read those books as I did.

DAVID COPPERFIELD

How should one esteem newspapers?

They are so filthy and bestial that no honest man would admit one into his house for a water-closet doormat.

LETTER TO HENRY AUSTIN

Is it true that everything in the press is to be believed, without question?

Even the Press, being human, may be sometimes mistaken or misinformed, and I rather think that I have in one or two rare instances observed its information to be not strictly accurate with reference to myself. Indeed, I have, now and again, been more surprised by printed news that I have read of myself, than by any printed news that I have ever read in my present state of existence.

MARTIN CHUZZLEWIT, POSTSCRIPT

How may one discuss the ability
to read and write without
causing offence?

'And yet you can read. And write
too, I shouldn't wonder?'

'Yes, ma'am,' said the child, fearful of
giving new offence by the confession.

'Well, and what a thing that is,'
returned Mrs Jarley. 'I can't!'

Nell said 'indeed' in a tone which might imply,
either that she was reasonably surprised to
find the genuine and only Jarley, who was
the delight of the Nobility and Gentry and
the peculiar pet of the Royal Family, destitute
of these familiar arts; or that she presumed
so great a lady could scarcely stand in need
of such ordinary accomplishments.

THE OLD CURIOSITY SHOP

Philosophical Thoughts

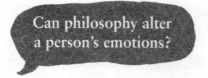

Can philosophy alter a person's emotions?

Mr Pickwick was a philosopher, but philosophers are only men in armour, after all. The shaft had reached him, penetrated through his philosophical harness, to his very heart. In the frenzy of his rage, he hurled the inkstand madly forward, and followed it up himself. But Mr Jingle had disappeared, and he found himself caught in the arms of Sam.

'Hollo,' said that eccentric functionary, 'furniter's cheap where you come from, Sir. Self-acting ink, that 'ere; it's wrote your mark upon the wall, old gen'l'm'n. Hold still, Sir; wot's the use o' runnin' arter a man as has made his lucky, and got to t'other end of the Borough by this time?'

Mr Pickwick's mind, like those of all truly great men, was open to conviction. He was a quick and powerful reasoner; and a moment's reflection sufficed to remind him of the impotency of his rage. It subsided as quickly as it had been roused. He panted for breath, and looked benignantly round upon his friends.

THE PICKWICK PAPERS

> Is love enough, or does the soul require testing to prove itself worthy of its love?

'And lastly, if you would like to know in confidence, as perhaps you may, what is my opinion of my husband, my opinion is – that I almost love him!'

'And if you would like to know in confidence, as perhaps you may,' said her husband, smiling, as he stood by her side, without her having detected his approach, 'my opinion of my wife, my opinion is —' But Bella started up, and put her hand upon his lips.

'Stop, Sir! No, John, dear! Seriously! Please not yet a while! I want to be something so much worthier than the doll in the doll's house.'

'My darling, are you not?'

'Not half, not a quarter, so much worthier as I hope you may some day find me! Try me through some reverse, John – try me through some trial – and tell them after THAT, what you think of me.'

'I will, my Life,' said John. 'I promise it.'

OUR MUTUAL FRIEND, BELLA AND JOHN ROKESMITH

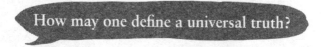

How may one define a universal truth?

'It was as true,' said Mr Barkis, 'as
turnips is. It was as true… as taxes is.
And nothing's truer than them.'

DAVID COPPERFIELD, MR BARKIS

> What is the most beautiful
> time of year?

There is no month in the whole year in which
nature wears a more beautiful appearance
than in the month of August. Spring has many
beauties, and May is a fresh and blooming
month, but the charms of this time of year are
enhanced by their contrast with the winter
season. August has no such advantage. It
comes when we remember nothing but clear
skies, green fields, and sweet-smelling flowers
– when the recollection of snow, and ice, and
bleak winds, has faded from our minds as
completely as they have disappeared from the
earth – and yet what a pleasant time it is!

THE PICKWICK PAPERS

How well can one person know another?

A wonderful fact to reflect upon, that every human creature is constituted to be that profound secret and mystery to every other… Something of the awfulness, even of Death itself, is referable to this. No more can I turn the leaves of this dear book that I loved, and vainly hope in time to read it all. No more can I look into the depths of this unfathomable water, wherein, as momentary lights glanced into it, I have had glimpses of buried treasure and other things submerged.

A TALE OF TWO CITIES

What is the sentiment of true chivalry?

'Women, after all, gentlemen,' said the enthusiastic Mr Snodgrass, 'are the great props and comforts of our existence.'

'So they are,' said the placid gentleman.

'When they're in a good humour,' interposed the dirty-faced man.

'And that's very true,' said the placid one.

'I repudiate that qualification,' said Mr Snodgrass, whose thoughts were fast reverting to Emily Wardle. 'I repudiate it with disdain – with indignation. Show me the man who says anything against women, as women, and I boldly declare he is not a man.' And Mr Snodgrass took his cigar from his mouth, and struck the table violently with his clenched fist.

THE PICKWICK PAPERS

> How are one's feelings and one's perceptions of the outside world connected?

Oliver rose next morning, in better heart, and went about his usual occupations, with more hope and pleasure than he had known for many days. The birds were once more hung out, to sing, in their old places; and the sweetest wild flowers that could be found, were once more gathered to gladden Rose with their beauty. The melancholy which had seemed to the sad eyes of the anxious boy to hang, for days past, over every object, beautiful as all were, was dispelled by magic. The dew seemed to sparkle more brightly on the green leaves; the air to rustle among them with a sweeter music; and the sky itself to look more blue and bright. Such is the influence which the condition of our own thoughts, exercise, even over the appearance of external objects. Men who look on nature, and their fellow-men, and cry that all is dark and gloomy, are in the right; but the sombre colours are reflections from their own jaundiced eyes and hearts. The real hues are delicate, and need a clearer vision.

OLIVER TWIST

How does an optimist
look at the world?

'Thank'ee, sir,' said Sam. And down he sat
without further bidding, having previously
deposited his old white hat on the landing outside
the door. ''Tain't a wery good 'un to look at,'
said Sam, 'but it's an astonishin' 'un to wear; and
afore the brim went, it was a wery handsome
tile. Hows'ever it's lighter without it, that's one
thing, and every hole lets in some air, that's
another – wentilation gossamer I calls it.' On
the delivery of this sentiment, Mr Weller smiled
agreeably upon the assembled Pickwickians.

THE PICKWICK PAPERS, SAM WELLER

> Can the way you look at the world
> actually alter the world you see?

'Well!' cried Mr Skimpole. 'You know the world (which in your sense is the universe), and I know nothing of it, so you shall have your way. But if I had mine,' glancing at the cousins, 'there should be no brambles of sordid realities in such a path as that. It should be strewn with roses; it should lie through bowers, where there was no spring, autumn, nor winter, but perpetual summer. Age or change should never wither it. The base word money should never be breathed near it!'

BLEAK HOUSE

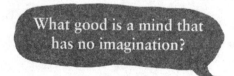

> What good is a mind that
> has no imagination?

Everything that Mr Smallweed's grandfather ever put away in his mind was a grub at first, and is a grub at last. In all his life he has never bred a single butterfly.

BLEAK HOUSE

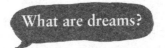

What are dreams?

Dreams are the bright creatures of poem and legend, who sport on earth in the night season, and melt away in the first beam of the sun, which lights grim care and stern reality on their daily pilgrimage through the world.

NICHOLAS NICKLEBY

Does fame always change
one's way of life?

I can't get down Broadway for my own
portrait; and yet I live almost as quietly in
this hotel, as if I were at the office, and go in
and out by a side door just as I might there.

LETTER TO MISS DICKENS, 30 DECEMBER 1867

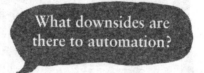

What downsides are
there to automation?

'I admire machinery as much as any man, and
am as thankful to it as any man can be for what
it does for us. But it will never be a substitute for
the face of a man, with his soul in it, encouraging
another man to be brave and true. Never try
it for that. It will break down like a straw.'

THE WRECK OF THE GOLDEN MARY,
WILLIAM GEORGE RAVENDER

The IMPROVED
PAT'D JULY 17, 1893
AND
APRIL 19, 1892.
PAN-AMERICAN
WASHER.

How can we explain the construction
of Stonehenge and other ancient
British monuments?

We know, from examination of the great blocks
of which such buildings are made, that they
could not have been raised without the aid of
some ingenious machines, which are common
now, but which the ancient Britons certainly
did not use in making their own uncomfortable
houses. I should not wonder if the Druids, and
their pupils who stayed with them twenty years,
knowing more than the rest of the Britons, kept
the people out of sight while they made these
buildings, and then pretended that they built
them by magic. Perhaps they had a hand in the
fortresses too; at all events, as they were very
powerful, and very much believed in, and as they
made and executed the laws, and paid no taxes, I
don't wonder that they liked their trade. And, as
they persuaded the people the more Druids there
were, the better off the people would be, I don't
wonder that there were a good many of them. But
it is pleasant to think that there are no Druids,
now, who go on in that way, and pretend to carry
Enchanters' Wands and Serpents' Eggs – and of
course there is nothing of the kind, anywhere.

A CHILD'S HISTORY OF ENGLAND

What is a Druid to do when his believers lose their faith?

Above all, it was in the Roman time, and by means of Roman ships, that the Christian Religion was first brought into Britain, and its people first taught the great lesson that, to be good in the sight of God, they must love their neighbours as themselves, and do unto others as they would be done by. The Druids declared that it was very wicked to believe in any such thing, and cursed all the people who did believe it, very heartily. But, when the people found that they were none the better for the blessings of the Druids, and none the worse for the curses of the Druids, but, that the sun shone and the rain fell without consulting the Druids at all, they just began to think that the Druids were mere men, and that it signified very little whether they cursed or blessed. After which, the pupils of the Druids fell off greatly in numbers, and the Druids took to other trades.

A CHILD'S HISTORY OF ENGLAND

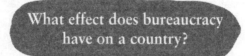

What effect does bureaucracy have on a country?

'Britannia, that unfortunate female, is always before me, like a trussed fowl: skewered through and through with office-pens, and bound hand and foot with red tape.'

DAVID COPPERFIELD, DAVID COPPERFIELD

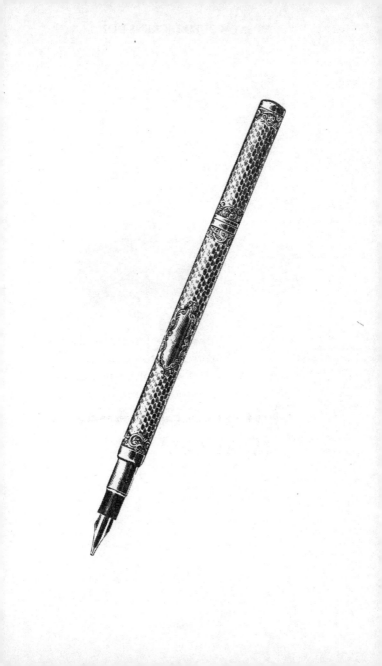

HONESTY – AND
DISHONESTY

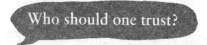

Who should one trust?

'You will not have forgotten that it was a maxim with Foxey – our revered father, gentlemen – "Always suspect everybody." That's the maxim to go through life with!'

THE OLD CURIOSITY SHOP, SAMPSON BRASS

Are people's names indicative of the type of people they are?

'He is well looking,' said Mr Pecksniff, slowly and distinctly; 'well looking enough. I do not positively expect any immediate premium with him.'

Notwithstanding their different natures, both Charity and Mercy concurred in opening their eyes uncommonly wide at this announcement, and in looking for the moment as blank as if their thoughts had actually had a direct bearing on the main chance.

MARTIN CHUZZLEWIT

How may discretion be ensured when
sharing secret information
with one's father?

'I'll tell you, Pa. I don't mind telling YOU, because
we have always been favourites of each other's,
and because you are not like a Pa, but more like
a sort of a younger brother with a dear venerable
chubbiness on him. And besides,' added Bella,
laughing as she pointed a rallying finger at his
face, 'because I have got you in my power. This is
a secret expedition. If ever you tell of me, I'll tell
of you. I'll tell Ma that you dined at Greenwich.'

'Well; seriously, my dear,' observed R.
W., with some trepidation of manner, 'it
might be as well not to mention it.'

'Aha!' laughed Bella. 'I knew you wouldn't
like it, sir! So you keep my confidence,
and I'll keep yours. But betray the lovely
woman, and you shall find her a serpent.'

OUR MUTUAL FRIEND, BELLA WILFER AND HER FATHER

Should people be believed when they tell you their age?

It was; for the infant phenomenon, though of short stature, had a comparatively aged countenance, and had moreover been precisely the same age – not perhaps to the full extent of the memory of the oldest inhabitant, but certainly for five good years. But she had been kept up late every night, and put upon an unlimited allowance of gin-and-water from infancy, to prevent her growing tall, and perhaps this system of training had produced in the infant phenomenon these additional phenomena.

NICHOLAS NICKLEBY

How much information should be taken on faith?

'Take nothing on its looks; take everything on evidence. There's no better rule.'

GREAT EXPECTATIONS, MR JAGGERS

HOW TO LIVE WELL

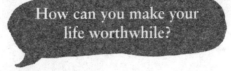

How can you make your
life worthwhile?

'I felt an earnest and humble desire,
and shall do till I die, to increase the
stock of harmless cheerfulness.'

SPEECH AT EDINBURGH, JUNE 25 1841

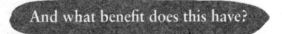

And what benefit does this have?

'No one is useless in this world,'
retorted the Secretary, 'who lightens
the burden of it for any one else.'

OUR MUTUAL FRIEND, JOHN ROKESMITH

What is the best way to make
a boring life interesting?

Change begets change. Nothing propagates so
fast. If a man habituated to a narrow circle of
cares and pleasures, out of which he seldom
travels, step beyond it, though for never so brief
a space, his departure from the monotonous
scene on which he has been an actor of
importance, would seem to be the signal for
instant confusion. As if, in the gap he had left,
the wedge of change were driven to the head,
rending what was a solid mass to fragments,
things cemented and held together by the usages
of years, burst asunder in as many weeks. The
mine which Time has slowly dug beneath familiar
objects is sprung in an instant; and what was
rock before, becomes but sand and dust.

MARTIN CHUZZLEWIT

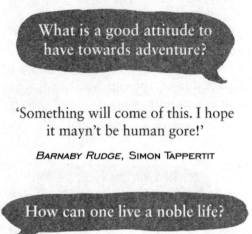

What is a good attitude to
have towards adventure?

'Something will come of this. I hope
it mayn't be human gore!'

BARNABY RUDGE, SIMON TAPPERTIT

How can one live a noble life?

'Never,' said my aunt, 'be mean in anything;
never be false; never be cruel. Avoid those three
vices, Trot, and I can always be hopeful of you.'

DAVID COPPERFIELD, BETSEY TROTWOOD

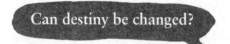

Can destiny be changed?

'Men's courses will foreshadow certain ends, to which, if persevered in, they must lead,' said Scrooge. 'But if the courses be departed from, the ends will change. Say it is thus with what you show me!'

A CHRISTMAS CAROL

What is a wasted life?

'If you could say, with truth, to your own solitary heart, to-night, "I have secured to myself the love and attachment, the gratitude or respect, of no human creature; I have won myself a tender place in no regard; I have done nothing good or serviceable to be remembered by!" your seventy-eight years would be seventy-eight heavy curses; would they not?'

A TALE OF TWO CITIES, SYDNEY CARTON

How should hard times in your past be looked upon?

Reflect upon your present blessings – of which every man has many – not on your past misfortunes, of which all men have some. Fill your glass again, with a merry face and contented heart.

SKETCHES BY BOZ

And what about current hard times?

'Under an accumulation of staggerers, no man can be considered a free agent. No man knocks himself down; if his destiny knocks him down, his destiny must pick him up again.'

THE OLD CURIOSITY SHOP, DICK SWIVELLER

www.summersdale.com